P9-ELR-338

SPRING BROOK ELEMENTARY
LIBRARY MEDIA CENTER
NAPERVILLE, IL 60565

Biographies

Madam C. J. Walker

Pioneer Businesswoman

by Katherine Krohn

Consultant:
A'Lelia Bundles
Great-great-granddaughter of Madam C. J. Walker
Author of *On Her Own Ground: The Life and Times of Madam C. J. Walker*

SPRING BROOK ELEMENTARY
LIBRARY MEDIA CENTER
NAPERVILLE, IL 60565

Capstone
press

Mankato, Minnesota

Fact Finders is published by Capstone Press,
151 Good Counsel Drive, P.O. Box 669, Mankato, Minnesota 56002.
www.capstonepress.com

Copyright © 2006 by Capstone Press. All rights reserved.
No part of this publication may be reproduced in whole or in part, or stored in a retrieval
system, or transmitted in any form or by any means, electronic, mechanical, photocopying,
recording, or otherwise, without written permission of the publisher.
For information regarding permission, write to Capstone Press,
151 Good Counsel Drive, P.O. Box 669, Dept. R, Mankato, Minnesota 56002.
Printed in the United States of America

Library of Congress Cataloging-in-Publication Data
Krohn, Katherine E.
    Madam C. J. Walker: Pioneer businesswoman / by Katherine Krohn.
    p. cm.—(Fact finders. Biographies)
    Includes bibliographical references and index.
    ISBN 0-7368-4346-9 ((hardcover)
    1. Walker, C. J., Madam, 1867–1919—Juvenile literature. 2. African American women
executives—Biography—Juvenile literature. 3. Women millionaires—United States—
Biography—Juvenile literature. 4. Cosmetics industry—United States—History—Juvenile
literature. I. Title. II. Series.
HD9970.5.C672W3546 2006
338.7'66855'092—dc22   2004027191

Summary: An introduction to the life of Madam C. J. Walker, an African American
    businesswoman who started her own business making and selling hair care products.

Editorial Credits
Megan Schoeneberger and Roberta Basel, editors; Juliette Peters, set designer; Patrick D.
    Dentinger, book designer and illustrator; Kelly Garvin, photo researcher/photo editor

Photo Credits
A'Lelia Bundles/Walker Family Collection, cover, 1, 5, 6–7, 13, 15, 17, 20, 24–25, 26, 27
Getty Images Inc./Hulton Archive, 9, 12
Library of Congress, 10–11, 19
Madam C. J. Walker Collection, Indiana Historical Society, 21
Museum of the City of New York, the Byron Collection, 23

1 2 3 4 5 6 10 09 08 07 06 05

Table of Contents

Chapter 1

Strong Woman

In 1912, nearly 2,000 people listened as Madam C. J. Walker began to speak. "I . . . came from the cotton fields of the South," she said. She told the crowd how no one had believed she could start a business. "But I know how to grow hair as well as I know how to grow cotton."

Walker was at a large meeting in Chicago, Illinois, for African American businesspeople. Walker told them about her hair care products for African Americans. She explained her plan to use her money to help other African Americans. The people clapped and cheered. The next year, Walker was asked to speak at the meeting again.

Madam C. J. Walker posed for this photograph in 1910.

Chapter 2

Early Years

On December 23, 1867, a baby girl was born to Owen and Minerva Breedlove. They named her Sarah. Many years later, she would change her name to Madam C. J. Walker.

Family Life

Walker grew up on a large cotton **plantation** in Delta, Louisiana. She lived in a one-room cabin with her parents, her sister, and her four brothers.

Walker's parents and older siblings had been slaves. The man who owned the plantation also had owned Walker's family. Two years before Walker was born, all slaves in the United States were set free.

Walker was born in this small cabin in 1867.

Walker and her family worked as **sharecroppers** on the plantation. The plantation owner gave them seeds and tools. In return, the Breedloves gave him part of the crop.

Walker helped her family by doing many chores. She helped her mother and sister, Louvenia, wash clothes. Walker fed the farm animals and picked cotton. She also carried buckets of water to the fields.

FACT!

Walker couldn't go to school. At that time, laws said that schools for black children and white children had to be separate. There were no schools for black children in Walker's town.

Changes

In the mid-1870s, Walker's life changed. Her mother died in 1873. Two years later, her father died. Her brothers left home to find jobs. Walker went to live with her sister. Louvenia's husband, Jesse Powell, treated Walker badly.

When Walker was 11, she and the Powells moved to Vicksburg, Mississippi. Walker got a job as a washerwoman. At that time, there were no laws stopping children from working. Walker washed white people's clothes. She gave the Powells the few pennies she earned each week.

QUOTE

"If I have accomplished anything in life it is because I have been willing to work hard."
—Madam C. J. Walker

Washerwomen like Walker cleaned other people's clothing by hand in large tubs. ▼

Chapter 3

Hard Times

In 1881, Walker married Moses McWilliams. She was 14 years old. In 1885, Walker and her husband had a baby girl and named her Lelia. Three years later, McWilliams died of unknown causes. Walker was left to raise Lelia by herself.

St. Louis

In early 1889, Walker decided to move to St. Louis, Missouri. Her brothers worked as barbers there. Walker and Lelia took a riverboat up the Mississippi River. Their beds were on the lower deck of the ship. Cows and chickens slept nearby. The weeklong trip was hot and smelly.

This photograph shows the Mississippi River near St. Louis in 1905. Like Walker, many people arrived in St. Louis on boats from cities along the river.

In St. Louis, Walker found a place to live in the poor part of town. She rented a small, unheated room. Walker got a job washing clothes. She earned about $1.50 a day.

On Sundays, Walker took a break from her hard work. She attended St. Paul African Methodist Episcopal Church. The members of the church became like a family to Walker. Through the church, Walker found out about a nearby school for African Americans. Lelia started first grade there in 1890.

This photograph shows St. Louis in 1890, the time when Walker lived there. ▼

A few years later, Walker met a man named John Davis. He had just moved to St. Louis from De Soto, Missouri. Walker and Davis were married in 1894.

Walker continued to work as a washerwoman. She worked very hard and saved her money. Walker wanted her daughter to get a good education. In 1902, she sent Lelia to Knoxville College in Tennessee.

▲ Lelia posed for this picture in 1913.

FACT!

While her daughter was in college, Walker decided to get an education too. She took reading, geography, and other classes at a night school in St. Louis.

Chapter 4

A New Job

In the early 1900s, Walker went to see a **hairdresser** named Annie Pope-Turnbo. Walker was worried about her hair. It had started to fall out a few years earlier. Pope-Turnbo sold shampoo and other hair products she made herself. She gave Walker a **scalp treatment**.

The women became friends. Walker started to work for Pope-Turnbo. She walked from house to house, selling shampoo and giving scalp treatments.

Walker liked her new job. She made more money than she had made washing clothes. But she wasn't happy in her marriage. Her husband didn't treat her well. In 1903, she left him.

This photograph of Walker from the 1890s shows her hair in poor condition.

QUOTE

"I had little or no opportunity
when I started out in life . . .
I had to make my own living
and my own opportunity."
—Madam C. J. Walker

A New Start

In 1905, Walker decided to leave St. Louis. She wanted to help African American women with hair problems in other parts of the country. She decided to move to Denver, Colorado.

Walker rented the attic of a house. She got a job as a cook in a **boarding house**. She also sold hair products for Pope-Turnbo. But Walker wanted to make her own products.

One night, Walker had a dream. In the dream, a large, dark-skinned man told her the ingredients for a special hair treatment.

Her Own Business

Walker mixed the ingredients together until she had the right recipe for a hair treatment. She used it on her hair. Before long, her hair began to grow back.

Walker took her product from house to house. She knocked on people's doors and **demonstrated** her "Wonderful Hair Grower." The treatment worked, and people wanted to buy it.

Walker sold her hair grower in round tins with her photograph on them. ▶

Chapter 5

Rising Star

Walker had kept in touch with a man she dated in St. Louis. Charles Joseph "C. J." Walker was a charming, well-dressed man who worked for a newspaper. Walker told C. J. about her new life in Denver. He decided to join her. Walker and C. J. married on January 4, 1906. She became known as Madam C. J. Walker.

Walker added shampoos and scalp treatments to the list of products she sold. She and Lelia traveled the United States, demonstrating Walker hair products. Back home, orders filled their mailbox. Money poured into Madam Walker's bank account.

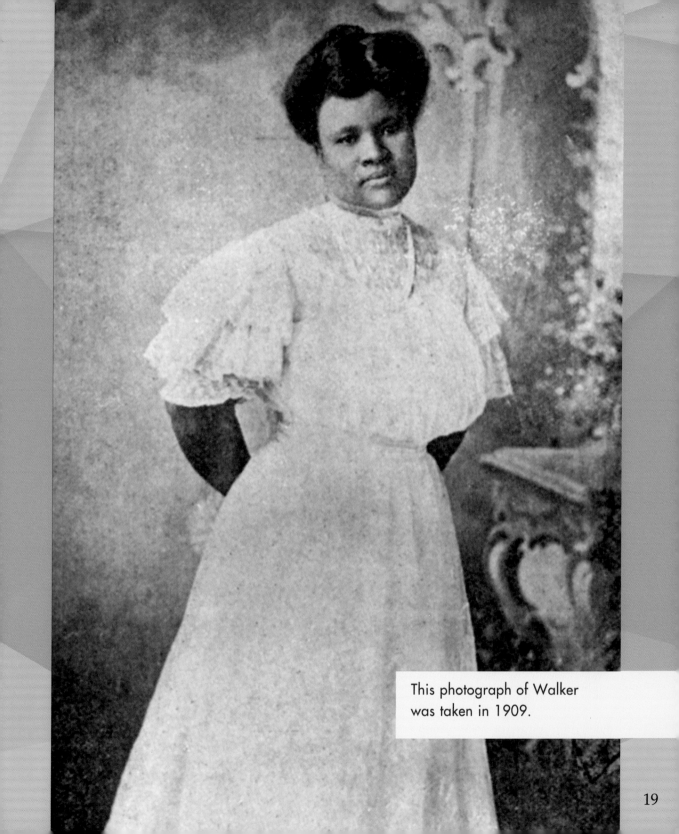

This photograph of Walker was taken in 1909.

A New College

In 1908, Walker moved her company to Pittsburgh, Pennsylvania. There, she opened a training school called Lelia College.

Lelia College trained hundreds of women to be Walker **Agents**. Walker taught them how to be hairdressers. They used Walker's products in their stores. If women could not go to the college, Walker offered the hairdressing class through the mail.

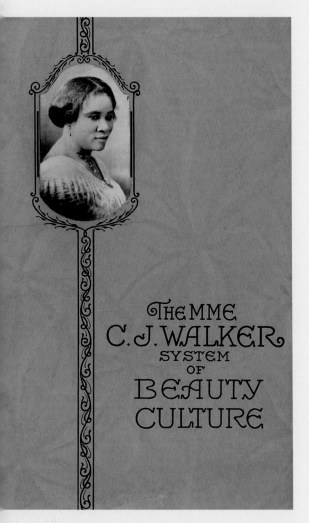

◀ Walker Agents received books like this one to learn her system for treating hair.

More Changes

In 1910, Walker moved to Indianapolis, Indiana. She opened another training school there. She also built a factory to make her hair products.

Walker's business was doing well. But her marriage wasn't happy. Walker and her husband disagreed on how to run the business. They divorced in 1912.

Walker's life was changing in other ways too. In 1912, Lelia adopted a 13-year-old girl named Fairy Mae Bryant. Walker was now a grandmother.

QUOTE

"I have made it possible for many colored women to abandon the washtub for more pleasant and profitable occupation."
—Madam C. J. Walker

Walker built a large home in Indianapolis. ▼

QUOTE

"I love to use a part of
what I make in trying to
help others."
—Madam C. J. Walker

In 1916, Walker moved again, this time to New York City. Lelia had moved there three years earlier.

Walker and Lelia bought a home in an area called Harlem. Harlem was a neighborhood with a large black population. Walker put a new Lelia College in the bottom floor of the house. She continued to travel the world, train agents, and sell her products.

Walker was very generous. She gave money to schools, orphanages, African American groups, and other charities.

↑ The lobby of the Lelia College in Harlem featured expensive furniture.

Chapter 6

Final Years

By the late 1910s, the Walker business was booming. Walker had money to spend on whatever she wished. But her health began to fail in late 1917. Her doctor told her she had heart problems. He told her to rest. But Walker had trouble resting. Her mind was always racing with ideas and plans for her company.

On May 25, 1919, Madam C. J. Walker died. She was 51 years old.

Even without Walker, the company kept going. Lelia took over until she died in 1931. Over the years, sales slowed. In 1985, the company was sold.

Walker (driving) earned enough money to buy fancy clothes and cars.

▲ Hundreds of Walker Agents gathered at Walker's mansion for a convention in 1924.

FACT!

In 1998, the U.S. Postal Service honored Walker on a postage stamp. The stamp was a part of the Black Heritage Series.

Walker's Legacy

Walker turned her idea for hair care products into a big business. She used her success to help others. Her products gave people healthy, beautiful hair. She also gave jobs to thousands of black women. Her employees worked as Walker Agents, factory workers, managers, and instructors. Walker helped many African American women live better lives. She inspired many others to succeed in business.

Fast Facts

Full name: Sarah Breedlove McWilliams Davis Walker; known as Madam C. J. Walker

Birth: December 23, 1867

Death: May 25, 1919

Hometown: Delta, Louisiana

Parents: Owen and Minerva Breedlove

Siblings: sister Louvenia; brothers Owen Jr., Alexander, James, Solomon

Husbands: Moses McWilliams; John Davis; Charles Joseph Walker

Daughter: Lelia

Education: night classes in St. Louis

Achievement: Founded the Madam C. J. Walker Manufacturing Company

Time Line

Life Events of Madam C. J. Walker

Walker is born December 23 in Delta, Louisiana.

Walker's hair begins to fall out.

| | 1867 | 1890s |

| 1861 | 1865 | |

Events in U.S. History

The Civil War begins.

The Civil War ends; Congress passes the 13th Amendment, which ends slavery in the United States.

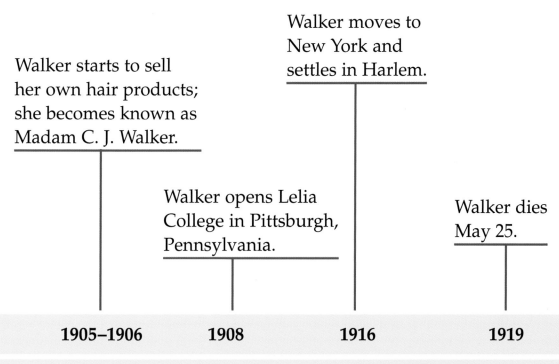

Walker starts to sell her own hair products; she becomes known as Madam C. J. Walker.

Walker moves to New York and settles in Harlem.

Walker opens Lelia College in Pittsburgh, Pennsylvania.

Walker dies May 25.

1905–1906   **1908**   **1916**   **1919**

1909   **1914–1918**

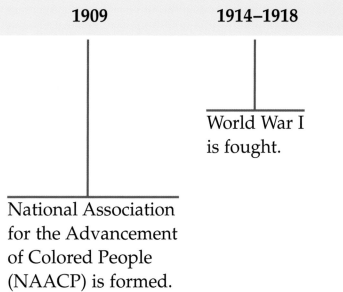

World War I is fought.

National Association for the Advancement of Colored People (NAACP) is formed.

Glossary

agent (AY-juhnt)—someone who arranges or sells things for other people

boarding house (BORD-ing HOWS)—a home that people pay to live in for a short time

demonstrate (DEM-uhn-strate)—to show other people how to do something or use something

hairdresser (HAIR-dress-ur)—a person who cuts or styles people's hair

plantation (plan-TAY-shuhn)—a large farm used for growing rubber, cotton, or other crops to sell

scalp treatment (SKALP TREET-muhnt)—a substance put on the head to help heal sores

sharecropper (SHAIR-krop-ur)—a person who farms a piece of land and pays the owner of the land with part of the crop or with money from the crops raised

Internet Sites

FactHound offers a safe, fun way to find Internet sites related to this book. All of the sites on FactHound have been researched by our staff.

Here's how:

1. Visit *www.facthound.com*
2. Type in this special code **0736843469** for age-appropriate sites. Or enter a search word related to this book for a more general search.
3. Click on the **Fetch It** button.

FactHound will fetch the best sites for you!

Read More

Bundles, A'Lelia Perry. *Madam C. J. Walker.* Black Americans of Achievement. New York: Chelsea House, 1991.

Hall, M.C. *Madam C. J. Walker.* Lives and Times. Chicago: Heinemann Library, 2003.

Hobkirk, Lori. *Madam C. J. Walker.* Journey to Freedom. Chanhassen, Minn.: Child's World, 2001.

Index